How to Keep Track to Get Out of Debt

This debt tracking book will help you keep track of all your bills and payments. With this easy to use 12-month organizer you can eliminate the need of keeping statements around the house. Everything you need is contained in this book.

Written by

Tabitha Donald

Tabitha Donald

How to Keep Track to Get Out of Debt

Copyright © 2013 Tabitha Donald

All rights reserved. No part of this book may be reproduced or transmitted in any format by any means without written permission from the publisher and author.

ISBN - 10: 1494455250
ISBN - 13: 978-1494455255

Published by Tabitha Donald through Createspace.com.

Tabitha Donald can be connected with through Facebook, Linkedin, Twitter, and at serena0924@hotmail.com.

DEDICATION

To my son, Timothy J. Donald. Keep God first and learn all you can to be successful in all areas of your life and most importantly, avoid overspending.

Mommy loves you very much.

CONTENTS

	Acknowledgments	vii
1	Prosperity Scriptures	9
2	Tracking Charts	10
3	Charitable Tracker	76-77
4	Hints for Accuracy	78

ACKNOWLEDGMENTS

I would like to convey my gratitude to several people who encouraged me to publish this book.

My husband, Derrick T. Donald, my biggest supporter. Thank you for your prayers and encouragement through this experience. Thank you for the time off to complete this book. I really needed the break and the free time. I love you so very, very much.

My son, Timothy Donald, if I can do it you can too. Never give up on your dreams. You will succeed.

My mom, Etheldra Stokes, thank you for your prayers and encouragement. I love you so much.

My grandma, Iola Alexander, for your wisdom when it comes to money. I've heard everything you said.

Lastly, to my godmother, Anita Dennis. You have been an answer to my prayers. Thank you for guiding me to a place where I could get my book published. I'm eternally grateful.

Thank you God for the inspiration and talent.

PROSPERITY SCRIPTURES

- Jeremiah 29:11 - For I know the thoughts that I think toward you, saith the LORD, thoughts of peace, and not of evil, to give you an expected end.
- Deuteronomy 8:18 - But thou shalt remember the LORD thy God: for it is he that giveth thee power to get wealth, that he may establish his covenant which he swore unto thy fathers, as it is this day.
- 3 John 1:2 - Beloved, I wish above all things that thou mayest prosper and be in health, even as thy soul prospereth.
- Psalms 1:3 - And he shall be like a tree planted by the rivers of water, that bringeth forth his fruit in his season; his leaf also shall not wither; and whatsoever he doeth shall prosper
- Hebrews 11:6 - And without faith, it is impossible to please God, because anyone who comes to Him must believe that he exists and that He rewards those who earnestly seek Him.
- 2 Corinthians 1:20 - For all the promises of God in Him are Yes, and in Him Amen, to the glory of God through us.
- Psalm 84:11-12 - For the Lord God is a sun and shield: the Lord will give grace and glory: no good thing will he withhold from them that walk uprightly.
- Psalm 85:12 - Yea, the Lord shall give that which is good; and our land shall yield her increase.
- Proverbs 10:27 - The blessing of the Lord brings wealth, and he adds no trouble to it.
- Deuteronomy 28:6 - Blessed shall you be when you come in, and blessed shall you be when you go out.

TRACKER

Company & # _____
Mailing address/Website _____
Contact name _____ File # _____
Payment amount _____ To be paid o Weekly o **Bi-weekly** o Monthly

	J	F	M	A	M	J	J	A	S	O	N	D
Date Paid												
Date Paid												
Date Paid												
Date Paid												
Interest /Late Fee												
Amt Paid												
Balance												
Debit/ Credit Card												
Check MO #												
Confir- mation												

Romans 13:8 "Let no debt remain outstanding, except the continuing debt to love one another, for whoever loves others has fulfilled the law."

Notes:

_____
_____
_____
_____
_____
_____
_____
_____
_____
_____
_____
_____
_____
_____
_____
_____
_____
_____
_____
_____

Don't Give Up. See it to the end.

Company & # _____
Mailing address/Website _____
Contact name _____ File # _____
Payment amount _____ To be paid ○ Weekly ○ Bi-weekly ○ Monthly

	J	F	M	A	M	J	J	A	S	O	N	D
Date Paid												
Date Paid												
Date Paid												
Date Paid												
Interest/ Late Fee												
Amt Paid												
Balance												
Debit/ Credit Card												
Check or MO #												
Confirmation												

Proverbs 21:20 "The wise man saves for the future but the foolish man spends whatever he gets."

Notes:

Keep Pressing your way through.

Company & # _____
Mailing address/Website _____
Contact name _____ File # _____
Payment amount _____ To be paid ○ Weekly ○ Bi-weekly ○ Monthly

	J	F	M	A	M	J	J	A	S	O	N	D
Date Paid												
Date Paid												
Date Paid												
Date Paid												
Interest/ Late Fee												
Amt Paid												
Balance												
Debit/ Credit Card												
Check or MO #												
Confir- mation												

Philippians 4:19 "My God will supply all your needs according to His riches in glory in Christ Jesus."

Note:
_____
_____
_____
_____
_____
_____
_____
_____
_____
_____
_____
_____
_____
_____
_____
_____
_____
_____
_____
_____
_____

No matter how hard it is, you are seeing a breakthrough.

Company & # _____
Mailing address/Website _____
Contact name _____ File # _____
Payment amount _____ To be paid ○ Weekly ○ Bi-weekly ○ Monthly

	J	F	M	A	M	J	J	A	S	O	N	D
Date Paid												
Date Paid												
Date Paid												
Date Paid												
Interest/ Late Fee												
Amt Paid												
Balance												
Debit/ Credit Card												
Check or MO #												
Confir- mation												

Proverbs 22:7 "The rich rules over the poor, and the borrower [is] servant to the lender."

Notes:

No matter how bad you messed up, you can overcome.

Company & # _____
Mailing address/Website _____
Contact name _____ File # _____
Payment amount _____ To be paid ○ Weekly ○ Bi-weekly ○ Monthly

	J	F	M	A	M	J	J	A	S	O	N	D
Date Paid												
Date Paid												
Date Paid												
Date Paid												
Interest/ Late Fee												
Amt Paid												
Balance												
Debit/ Credit Card												
Check or MO #												
Confir- mation												

Romans 13:8 "Owe no man anything, but to love one another: for he that loveth another hath fulfilled the law."

Notes:

Nothings too hard for God.

Company & # _____
Mailing address/Website _____
Contact name _____ File # _____
Payment amount _____ To be paid ○ Weekly ○ Bi-weekly ○ Monthly

	J	F	M	A	M	J	J	A	S	O	N	D
Date Paid												
Date Paid												
Date Paid												
Date Paid												
Interest/Late Fee												
Amt Paid												
Balance												
Debit/Credit Card												
Check or MO #												
Confirmation												

Matthew 6:33 "But seek ye first the kingdom of God, and his righteousness; and all these things shall be added unto you."

Notes:

Don't worry, turn it over to God. He will work it out.

Company & # _____
Mailing address/Website_____
Contact name _____ File # _____
Payment amount _____ To be paid ○ Weekly ○ Bi-weekly ○ Monthly

	J	F	M	A	M	J	J	A	S	O	N	D
Date Paid												
Date Paid												
Date Paid												
Date Paid												
Interest/ Late Fee												
Amt Paid												
Balance												
Debit/ Credit Card												
Check or MO #												
Confirmation												

Ecclesiastes 5:5 "Better [is it] that thou shouldest not vow, than that thou shouldest vow and not pay."

Notes:

Do your best and let God do the rest.

Company & # _____
Mailing address/Website_____
Contact name _____ File # _____
Payment amount _____ To be paid ○ Weekly ○ Bi-weekly ○ Monthly

	J	F	M	A	M	J	J	A	S	O	N	D
Date Paid												
Date Paid												
Date Paid												
Date Paid												
Interest/ Late Fee												
Amt Paid												
Balance												
Debit/ Credit Card												
Check or MO #												
Confir- mation												

John 10:10 "The thief cometh not, but for to steal, and to kill, and to destroy: I am come that they might have life, and that they might have it more abundantly."

Notes:

___

You never know if can succeed until you try.

Company & # _____
Mailing address/Website_____
Contact name _____ File # _____
Payment amount _____ To be paid ○ Weekly ○ Bi-weekly ○ Monthly

	J	F	M	A	M	J	J	A	S	O	N	D
Date Paid												
Date Paid												
Date Paid												
Interest/ Late Fee												
Amt Paid												
Balance												
Debit/ Credit Card												
Check or MO #												
Confir- mation												

Luke 16:19 "If therefore ye have not been faithful in the unrighteous mammon, who will commit to your trust the true riches?"

Notes:

Eliminating debt is a good feeling. Try it.

Company & # _____
Mailing address/Website_____
Contact name _____ File # _____
Payment amount _____ To be paid ○ Weekly ○ Bi-weekly ○ Monthly

	J	F	M	A	M	J	J	A	S	O	N	D
Date Paid												
Date Paid												
Date Paid												
Date Paid												
Interest/ Late Fee												
Amt Paid												
Balance												
Debit/ Credit Card												
Check or Mo #												
Confir- mation												

God calls the ants wise because they prepare their meat in the summer. Why can't we show a little of the same wisdom?

Notes:

No more debt = 0 stress.

Company & # _____
Mailing address/Website_____
Contact name _____ File # _____
Payment amount _____ To be paid ○ Weekly ○ Bi-weekly ○ Monthly

	J	F	M	A	M	J	J	A	S	O	N	D
Date Paid												
Date Paid												
Date Paid												
Date Paid												
Interest/ Late Fee												
Amt Paid												
Balance												
Debit/ Credit Card												
Check or MO #												
Confirmation												

Principle 1: If you spend more than you earn, you are going into debt or you are in debt.

Notes:

No more being a slave to the lender.

Company & # _____
Mailing address/Website_____
Contact name _____ File # _____
Payment amount _____ To be paid ○ Weekly ○ Bi-weekly ○ Monthly

	J	F	M	A	M	J	J	A	S	O	N	D
Date Paid												
Date Paid												
Date Paid												
Date Paid												
Interest/ Late Fee												
Amt Paid												
Balance												
Debit/ Credit Card												
Check or MO #												
Confir- mation												

Principle 2: If you continually spend more than what you earn, you are on your way into a major pit.

Notes:

Debt, you have to go.

Company & # _____
Mailing address/Website_____
Contact name _____ File # _____
Payment amount _____ To be paid ○ Weekly ○ Bi-weekly ○ Monthly

	J	F	M	A	M	J	J	A	S	O	N	D
Date Paid												
Date Paid												
Date Paid												
Date Paid												
Interest/ Late Fee												
Amt Paid												
Balance												
Debit/ Credit Card												
Check or MO #												
Confir- mation												

Principle 3: You need to increase your income or decrease what is going out.

Notes:

If you can't pay cash, you don't need it.

Company & # _____
Mailing address/Website_____
Contact name _____ File # _____
Payment amount _____ To be paid ○ Weekly ○ Bi-weekly ○ Monthly

	J	F	M	A	M	J	J	A	S	O	N	D
Date Paid												
Date Paid												
Date Paid												
Date Paid												
Interest/ Late Fee												
Amt Paid												
Balance												
Debit/ Credit Card												
Check or MO #												
Confir- mation												

Proverbs 3:5-6 "Trust in the LORD with all your heart; and lean not unto your own understanding. In all thy ways acknowledge him, and he shall direct thy paths."

Notes:

Overspending is not wise.

Company & # _____
Mailing address/Website_____
Contact name _____ File # _____
Payment amount _____ To be paid ○ Weekly ○ Bi-weekly ○ Monthly

	J	F	M	A	M	J	J	A	S	O	N	D
Date Paid												
Date Paid												
Date Paid												
Date Paid												
Interest/ Late Fee												
Amt Paid												
Balance												
Debit/ Credit Card												
Check or MO #												
Confir- mation												

Proverbs 19:17 "He that hath pity upon the poor lendeth unto the LORD; and that which he hath given will he pay him again."

Notes:

Don't avoid the calls just pay the bill.

Company & # _____
Mailing address/Website_____
Contact name _____ File # _____
Payment amount _____ To be paid ○ Weekly ○ Bi-weekly ○ Monthly

	J	F	M	A	M	J	J	A	S	O	N	D
Date Paid												
Date Paid												
Date Paid												
Date Paid												
Interest/ Late Fee												
Amt Paid												
Balance												
Debit/ Credit Card												
Check or MO #												
Confir- mation												

Webster Dictionary: Debt - 1. That which is due from one person to another or others, whether goods, money, or services; something owed. 2. An obligation or liability to pay or return something. 3. The condition of being under obligation to pay money to, or perform services for, another.

Notes:

Paying something is better than paying nothing.

Company & # _____
Mailing address/Website_____
Contact name _____ File # _____
Payment amount _____ To be paid ○ Weekly ○ Bi-weekly ○ Monthly

	J	F	M	A	M	J	J	A	S	O	N	D
Date Paid												
Date Paid												
Date Paid												
Date Paid												
Interest/ Late Fee												
Amt Paid												
Balance												
Debit/ Credit Card												
Check or MO #												
Confir- mation												

Webster Dictionary: Owe - to have an obligation to pay; to be indebted to the amount of.

Notes:
_____

You will succeed as long as you don't give up.

Company & # _____
Mailing address/Website_____
Contact name _____ File # _____
Payment amount _____ To be paid ○ Weekly ○ Bi-weekly ○ Monthly

	J	F	M	A	M	J	J	A	S	O	N	D
Date Paid												
Date Paid												
Date Paid												
Date Paid												
Interest/ Late Fee												
Amt Paid												
Balance												
Debit/ Credit Card												
Check or MO #												
Confirmation												

Proverbs 10:4 "He becometh poor that dealeth [with] a slack hand: but the hand of the diligent makes rich."

Notes:

Spend wisely.

Company & # _____
Mailing address/Website_____
Contact name _____ File # _____
Payment amount _____ To be paid ○ Weekly ○ Bi-weekly ○ Monthly

	J	F	M	A	M	J	J	A	S	O	N	D
Date Paid												
Date Paid												
Date Paid												
Date Paid												
Interest/ Late Fee												
Amt Paid												
Balance												
Debit/ Credit Card												
Check or MO #												
Confir- mation												

Proverbs 10:22 "The blessing of the LORD, it maketh rich, and he addeth no sorrow with it."

Notes:

Strive to learn something new every day about being debt free.

Company & # _____
Mailing address/Website_____
Contact name _____ File # _____
Payment amount _____ To be paid ○ Weekly ○ Bi-weekly ○ Monthly

	J	F	M	A	M	J	J	A	S	O	N	D
Date Paid												
Date Paid												
Date Paid												
Date Paid												
Interest/ Late Fee												
Amt Paid												
Balance												
Debit/ Credit Card												
Check or MO #												
Confir-mation												

Job 22:21 "Submit to God and be at peace with him; in this way prosperity will come to you."

Notes:

Debt = burden, so get rid of it.

Company & # _____
Mailing address/Website_____
Contact name _____ File # _____
Payment amount _____ To be paid ○ Weekly ○ Bi-weekly ○ Monthly

	J	F	M	A	M	J	J	A	S	O	N	D
Date Paid												
Date Paid												
Date Paid												
Date Paid												
Interest/ Late Fee												
Amt Paid												
Balance												
Debit/ Credit Card												
Check or MO #												
Confir- mation												

Jeremiah 29:11 "For I know the plans I have for you," declares the Lord, "plans to prosper you and not to harm you, plans to give you hope and a future."

Notes:

In the name of Jesus, debt you got to go.

Company & # _____
Mailing address/Website_____
Contact name _____ File # _____
Payment amount _____ To be paid ○ Weekly ○ Bi-weekly ○ Monthly

	J	F	M	A	M	J	J	A	S	O	N	D
Date Paid												
Date Paid												
Date Paid												
Date Paid												
Interest/ Late Fee												
Amt Paid												
Balance												
Debit/ Credit Card												
Check or MO #												
Confir- mation												

Psalm 85:12 - Yea, the Lord shall give that which is good; and our land shall yield her increase.

Notes:

Every payment made is a step towards victory.

Company & # _____
Mailing address/Website_____
Contact name _____ File # _____
Payment amount _____ To be paid ○ Weekly ○ Bi-weekly ○ Monthly

	J	F	M	A	M	J	J	A	S	O	N	D
Date Paid												
Date Paid												
Date Paid												
Date Paid												
Interest/ Late Fee												
Amt Paid												
Balance												
Debit/ Credit Card												
Check or MO #												
Confirmation												

Romans 13:8 "Let no debt remain outstanding, except the continuing debt to love one another, for whoever loves others has fulfilled the law."

Notes:

Praise God in advance for your victory from debt.

Company & # _____
Mailing address/Website_____
Contact name _____ File # _____
Payment amount _____ To be paid ○ Weekly ○ Bi-weekly ○ Monthly

	J	F	M	A	M	J	J	A	S	O	N	D
Date Paid												
Date Paid												
Date Paid												
Date Paid												
Interest/ Late Fee												
Amt Paid												
Balance												
Debit/ Credit Card												
Check or MO #												
Confir- mation												

Proverbs 21:20 "The wise man saves for the future but the foolish man spends whatever he gets."

Notes:

Breaking the chains of bondage called debt.

Company & # _____
Mailing address/Website_____
Contact name _____ File # _____
Payment amount _____ To be paid ○ Weekly ○ Bi-weekly ○ Monthly

	J	F	M	A	M	J	J	A	S	O	N	D
Date Paid												
Date Paid												
Date Paid												
Date Paid												
Interest/ Late Fee												
Amt Paid												
Balance												
Debit/ Credit Card												
Check or MO #												
Confir- mation												

Philippians 4:19 "My God will supply all your needs according to His riches in glory in Christ Jesus."

Note:

When you get free from debt, stay free.

Company & # _____
Mailing address/Website_____
Contact name _____ File # _____
Payment amount _____ To be paid ○ Weekly ○ Bi-weekly ○ Monthly

	J	F	M	A	M	J	J	A	S	O	N	D
Date Paid												
Date Paid												
Date Paid												
Date Paid												
Interest/ Late Fee												
Amt Paid												
Balance												
Debit/ Credit Card												
Check or MO #												
Confir- mation												

Proverbs 22:7 "The rich rules over the poor, and the borrower [is] servant to the lender."

Notes:

Give out of your abundance not your need.

Company & # _____
Mailing address/Website _____
Contact name _____ File # _____
Payment amount _____ To be paid ○ Weekly ○ Bi-weekly ○ Monthly

	J	F	M	A	M	J	J	A	S	O	N	D
Date Paid												
Date Paid												
Date Paid												
Date Paid												
Interest/ Late Fee												
Amt Paid												
Balance												
Debit/ Credit Card												
Check or MO #												
Confir- mation												

Romans 13:8 "Owe no man anything, but to love one another: for he that loveth another hath fulfilled the law."

Notes:

The more you free up, the more you have to share with others.

Company & # _____
Mailing address/Website_____
Contact name _____ File # _____
Payment amount _____ To be paid ○ Weekly ○ Bi-weekly ○ Monthly

	J	F	M	A	M	J	J	A	S	O	N	D
Dare Paid												
Date Paid												
Date Paid												
Date Paid												
Interest/ Late Fee												
Amt Paid												
Balance												
Debit/ Credit Card												
Check or MO #												
Confir- mation												

Matthew 6:33 "But seek ye first the kingdom of God, and his righteousness; and all these things shall be added unto you."

Notes:

God wants you free from debt.

Company & # _____
Mailing address/Website_____
Contact name _____ File # _____
Payment amount _____ To be paid ○ Weekly ○ Bi-weekly ○ Monthly

	J	F	M	A	M	J	J	A	S	O	N	D
Date Paid												
Date Paid												
Date Paid												
Date Paid												
Interest/Late Fee												
Amt Paid												
Balance												
Debit/Credit Card												
Check or MO #												
Confirmation												

Ecclesiastes 5:5 "Better [is it] that thou shouldest not vow, than that thou shouldest vow and not pay."

Notes:

God cares about your needs.

Company & # _____
Mailing address/Website_____
Contact name _____ File # _____
Payment amount _____ To be paid ○ Weekly ○ Bi-weekly ○ Monthly

	J	F	M	A	M	J	J	A	S	O	N	D
Date Paid												
Date Paid												
Date Paid												
Date Paid												
Interest/ Late Fee												
Amt Paid												
Balance												
Debit/ Credit Card												
Check or MO #												
Confir- mation												

John 10:10 "The thief cometh not, but for to steal, and to kill, and to destroy: I am come that they might have life, and that they might have it more abundantly."

Notes:

God wants his people to prosper and not be bound by debt.

Company & # _____
Mailing address/Website_____
Contact name _____ File # _____
Payment amount _____ To be paid ○ Weekly ○ Bi-weekly ○ Monthly

	J	F	M	A	M	J	J	A	S	O	N	D
Date Paid												
Date Paid												
Date Paid												
Date Paid												
Interest/ Late Fee												
Amt Paid												
Balance												
Debit/ Credit Card												
Check or MO #												
Confir- mation												

Luke 16:19 "If therefore ye have not been faithful in the unrighteous mammon, who will commit to your trust the true riches?"

Notes:

Jesus is a way maker. Seek him.

Company & # _____
Mailing address/Website_____
Contact name _____ File # _____
Payment amount _____ To be paid ○ Weekly ○ Bi-weekly ○ Monthly

	J	F	M	A	M	J	J	A	S	O	N	D
Date Paid												
Date Paid												
Date Paid												
Date Paid												
Interest/ Late Fee												
Amt Paid												
Balance												
Debit. Credit Card												
Check or MO #												
Confir- mation												

God calls the ants wise because they prepare their meat in the summer. Why can't we show a little of the same wisdom?

Notes:

God bless me with the ability and wisdom I need to get out of debt.

Company & # _____
Mailing address/Website_____
Contact name _____ File # _____
Payment amount _____ To be paid ○ Weekly ○ Bi-weekly ○ Monthly

	J	F	M	A	M	J	J	A	S	O	N	D
Date Paid												
Date Paid												
Date Paid												
Date Paid												
Interest/ Late Fee												
Amt Paid												
Balance												
Debit/ Credit Card												
Check or MO #												
Confir- mation												

Proverbs 3:5-6 "Trust in the LORD with all your heart; and lean not unto your own understanding. In all thy ways acknowledge him, and he shall direct thy paths."

Notes:

Stick with the plan, you will see results.

Charitable Giving Record

	J	F	M	A	M	J	J	A	S	O	N	D
1												
2												
3												
4												
5												
6												
7												
8												
9												
10												
11												
12												
13												
14												
15												
16												
17												
18												
19												
20												
21												
22												
23												
24												
25												
26												
27												
28												
29												

How to Keep Track to Get Out of Debt

30											
31											
Total											

Hints for accuracy

- Fill in all the blank lines so there is no guessing later.

- Be sure to write down contact person & phone number. You never know when you have to call them or refer to the person you spoke to in the past.

- The top row shows the letters J, F ,M, A, M, J, ,J, A, S, O, N, D. These letters represent the month (i.e. J – Jan, F – Feb, etc…).

- Be sure to write down any late fees, interest you accumulated, and check or money order numbers. You never know if you have to refer back later for payment information.

- If you make a payment by credit card be sure to write down the confirmation number.

- Be sure to use the notes section to jot down any additional information that you may need.

- Be neat and accurate.

Numbers 6:22-27 (NIV)

22 The Lord said to Moses, 23 "Tell Aaron and his sons, 'This is how you are to bless the Israelites. Say to them:

24 "The Lord bless you
and keep you;
25 the Lord make his face shine on you
and be gracious to you;
26 the Lord turn his face toward you
and give you peace."

27 "So they will put my name on the Israelites, and I will bless them."

Note: Keeping accurate records of payments and payments made is the first step in getting out of debt. This book is not intended to be the answer to all your financial problems. However, it's intended to be your financial assistant that will assist you in becoming debt free and staying debt free.

Proverbs 22:26-27 - Do not be a man who strikes hands in pledge or puts up security for debts; if you lack the means to pay, your very bed will be snatched from under you.

1 Peter 5:7 - Casting all your anxiety on Him, because He cares for you.

Proverbs 22:7 - The rich rules over the poor, and the borrower becomes the lender's slave.

Joshua 1:8 - This Book of the Law shall not depart from your mouth, but you shall meditate in it day and night, that you may observe to do according to all that is written in it. For then you will make your way prosperous, and then you will have good success.

Psalm 122:6 - Pray for the peace of Jerusalem: "May they prosper who love you.

Debt is a burden… Get rid of it.

How to Keep Track to Get Out of Debt

www.ingramcontent.com/pod-product-compliance
Lightning Source LLC
Chambersburg PA
CBHW071802200526
45167CB00017B/1060